PRACTICAL TIPS ON

How To
Contract

BY
LAURA FREDERICK

Practical Tips on How to Contract

Please contact Laura Frederick at laura@frederick.law with any questions or suggestions.

ABOUT LAURA FREDERICK

Laura Frederick is a technology and commercial transactions attorney with 25 years of experience drafting and negotiating contracts. She is the Managing Attorney at Laura Frederick Law PLLC, a boutique law firm based in Austin, Texas that helps businesses with their vendor contracts. She also is the Founder and President of Contract Mentors Group LLC, a training and consulting company that helps lawyers and professionals learn how to draft and negotiate contracts.

Laura spent most of her career explaining and training on contracts. But prior to 2020, she limited her advice to her clients and coworkers. In August 2020, she started sharing her insightful contract tips through daily posts on LinkedIn. She quickly developed a following of enthusiastic fans who look forward to her LinkedIn posts every day. Her followers include experienced attorneys, who use the posts to refresh their knowledge, and others who rely on her tips to learn the basics.

Laura Frederick had an impressive legal career that took her across the U.S. and around the globe. She spent her first three years of legal practice working at law firms on franchise and distribution agreements. She then moved into technology transactions, working at a firm that merged into what is now Fulbright Rose Norton. She later joined the international law firm of Morrison & Foerster and spent five years working in its Technology Transactions group. She was based in its San Francisco office for two years and its Hong Kong and Singapore offices for three. She left that firm to join PPL Corporation, a diversified energy company, where she led legal support for all commercial and intellectual property matters. In 2010, Laura began her work as in-house counsel at several solar power companies, including Amonix, Hanwha Q CELLS, and SolarCity. In early 2017, she joined Tesla as commercial attorney working on vendor contracts and global environmental commodity deals. She left Tesla in early 2019 to open her own firm, Laura Frederick Law.

Laura received her undergraduate degree from George Washington University in Washington, D.C., where she majored in International Economics. She then earned her law degree from Emory University School of Law in Atlanta, Georgia, which she attended on a full-tuition merit scholarship. Following law school, she was selected as a Fulbright Scholar and spent a year studying international commercial dispute resolution at the University of British Columbia School of Law in Vancouver, Canada.

Laura now lives in Austin, Texas with her husband, four teenage sons, and two rescue dogs.

Do the best you can until you know better. Then when you know better, do better.

- *Maya Angelou*

TABLE OF CONTENTS

INTRODUCTION

This book is a collection of the daily advice covering random contract topics that I shared on LinkedIn. Each page has a different contract tip. It does not provide comprehensive coverage of each topic.

This is not your typical legal advice book. There are no footnotes or case names. I reference a few statutes, but infrequently.

Instead, this book reflects what I know based on what I've learned over my career. I was privileged to train under some of the top commercial and technology lawyers in the U.S. My understanding of how contracts work also comes from my own experiences in law firms and businesses. I spent the last 25 years as a contract practioner. My contract tips come from that perspective.

Take what I say in these tips with some healthy skepticism. Contract drafting and negotiation is not a science. There are no universal absolute rules. All contract advice reflects the writer's opinions. Contracts are as diverse and complex as the world of people, businesses, and things in it. There is not one way to draft or negotiate contracts.

While many concepts about contracts apply around the world, I bring the perspective of a U.S. lawyer applying U.S. laws. My practice is limited to technology and commercial contracts, so my topics reflect that segment of contracts.

I welcome feedback from people who have different perspectives and experiences. I think the fact that we don't agree on some things is awesome. It allows us to explore what we each think so we can learn from each other.

I may be the author of my tips and this book, but I rely on all the feedback from readers to make it better. You can direct message me on LinkedIn. My profile is linkedin.com/in/laurafredericklaw. Together we can continue to expand our understanding of how to draft and negotiate contracts.

Laura Frederick
Austin, Texas
November 2020

CHAPTER 1

ADVISING CLIENTS

How to Figure Out Your Client's Priorities

This contract tip is about how to figure out your client's priorities.

You need to keep your client's desired outcome as the priority. But what if you don't know what that outcome is? Ideally, you should ask your client.

While this approach is the best way, sometimes it isn't an option. I've found some clients aren't able or lack the interest to explain them. Others may expect you to already know or figure them out yourself.

When I don't have input from the client or I sense there may be more than what the client described, I identify the priorities by looking at the nature of the transaction, the products, and the parties to the contract.

For sellers, the most common priorities are:

1. limit contract requirements to what it can do,

2. limit exposure if things go wrong, and

3. get paid in full and on time.

For buyers, the most common priorities are:

1. make sure the seller does what is needed,

2. make sure the seller resolves problems and stands behind the product, and

3. pay in full only if the product is delivered and works.

Make sure your contracts for commercial deals adequately cover these priorities even if the client doesn't tell you as much.

How to Think about the Vendor Contract Review Process

This contract tip highlights how to think about the vendor contract review process in the context of the bigger world of contracts.

A colleague years ago said that legal review of vendor contracts is like death by a thousand cuts.

I think most lawyers feel that way. And I get it.

We never have time to review them as we'd like. We must use less than perfect terms because of the counterparty's requirements. We can't fix all the problems in the contracts.

For me, that inherent chaos and imperfection is my favorite thing about vendor contracts.

Now I sometimes lead negotiation of mega commercial deals (including a few $1B+). Those are fun too in their own way. We have the luxury of amazing lawyers on both sides, sophisticated business teams who are focused and motivated, and (usually) both sides want to spend the time to get the contracts as perfect as we can make them.

But for the bulk of vendor contract work, we review and we triage. We spend time on the ones that need our attention the most and get the rest good enough to sign. We're like the MASH unit of the contract world. And for many of us, that is exactly why we love this work.

CHAPTER 2

ASSIGNMENT

Assignment and Novation

This contract tip is about assignment and novation.

Did you know that a party that assigns a contract remains bound by that contract? U.S. law is clear on this point. An assignment by itself does not end the assignor's obligations under a contract. The only way to release the assignor is to have all three parties - the assignor, the assignee, and the other party to the agreement - agree to a novation.

I recently had an attorney refuse an assignment provision that allowed the parties to assign to affiliates. The lawyer's argument was that my client "could just assign to a shell company" and then his client would have no recourse against anyone. That's not how it works.

A party to a contract cannot assign a contract and walk away from liability. It still is liable AFTER the assignment. The only way the assignor is off the hook is with a novation. There are other risks to allowing assignment without restriction, but this idea that the other party is left without recourse is not one of them.

I urge lawyers everywhere (but especially lawyers with whom I negotiate) to stop recycling this incorrect argument.

Assignment of Accounts Receivable

This contract tip is about assigning the accounts receivable under a contract.

There are several sections in the Uniform Commercial Code (UCC) in the U.S. that overrule the contract. One of those superseding sections is UCC's Section 9-406. If you do not know about Section 9-406, you need to.

This section says that the seller may assign its accounts receivable under a contract even when the contract prohibits it. In other words, a buyer cannot prevent its vendors from using the accounts receivable as collateral for a loan or from selling the account (a practice called factoring).

You may ask, "Why does this matter to me?" Here is why. If you receive a notice from your vendor that it assigned your account and directs you to pay that assignee, you must stop payments to the vendor and only pay the new assignee. If a buyer pays the vendor instead of the assignee after receiving a valid 9-406 notice, the buyer still must pay the assignee.

Freaked out? I was too when I learned about this rule.

Train your teams to send Legal any notice about a new payee. Legal should validate it for compliance with the UCC and then advise on the next steps. Otherwise, your company may find that it still owes an amount that it already paid.

CHAPTER 3

BUYING AND SELLING GOODS

Preparing a Contract to Buy or Sell Goods

This contract tip is about what you need to know to prepare a contract to buy or sell goods.

Always make sure you are clear on these three questions before you draft or review the contract:

1. How will the buyer use the good? Contracts for purchasing goods are different depending on the type of use planned. Is the buyer using the good to run tests in a lab, manufacture parts in a factory, or combine with other products for sale to consumers?

2. What type of business is the seller? All customers expect the seller to stand behind its goods, but the expectations are different depending on the seller's type of business. Is the seller merely a distributor of goods originating from unrelated third parties? Or is it or its affiliate is the manufacturer?

3. Are there any customizations? The design of the product and the source of those designs affects many provisions in contracts to purchase or sell goods. Make sure you know if it is off the shelf, custom-built with the seller's design, or custom-built with the buyer's design.

Seller's Obligation to Sell

This contract tip is about a seller's obligation to sell.

Many sales contracts require buyers to purchase a minimum quantity of products from the seller.

Contracts include these obligations as binding forecasts, minimum purchase requirements, or monthly payments for a minimum level of purchases.

While these contracts require the buyer to buy, they sometimes do not obligate the seller to sell. Check the ordering process section to see if the seller has an unrestricted right to reject the buyer's purchase orders.

The seller's right to reject purchase orders may not be a big deal if the buyer has many sources for the products. But it is a big deal if the seller is the sole source or is building a custom-built product for the buyer. In those cases, make sure to add language that requires the seller to accept all the buyer's purchase orders for the products.

If the seller has limited supply, you can limit the obligation to quantities in the buyer's forecast approved by the seller. If the buyer may need more than its forecast, add a range of orders that the seller must accept. This approach might read "Seller will accept all purchase orders for products up to 120% of the monthly forecasted volume."

When a Service Level Should Apply to a Good or Service

This contract tip is about when a service level should apply to a good or service.

Many contracts require products to meet performance standards. These standards have many names, including performance warranties, key performance indicators (KPIs), and service levels.

The contract identifies a metric - like availability, uptime, or output - and a consequence for the failure to meet the metric. "Seller will cause the Service to operate X% of the time" or "Seller guarantees that the Equipment will manufacture at least X units per hour."

If your contract has service levels, consider whether the performance metric should apply to the entire term of the contract. Using one metric for the contract term may work if the product is off-the-shelf and is fully operational as soon as it is installed or used.

But if the product or service requires implementation, commissioning, or customization, you might need to add a time buffer. You should include a time buffer of how much time you reasonably need to ramp up the product.

Take time to think through the operational and technical aspects of your deal. There is no one approach fits all when it comes to performance metrics.

CHAPTER 4

CONFIDENTIALITY AND NDAs

Overlap of the Terms Proprietary, Confidential, and Trade Secret

This contract tip covers the overlap of the terms proprietary, confidential, and trade secret.

Proprietary and confidential do not have an accepted legal meaning other than the plain English definitions. Proprietary means something owned. Confidential means something secret.

In contrast, trade secret is a statutory term. The exact definition depends on which statute you read, but it typically is information not generally known to the public that has economic value because it is not known and that the owner takes reasonable steps to keep secret.

Looking at how they overlap helps me keep these terms clear.

Trade secrets are both proprietary (you own rights in your trade secrets) and confidential (it isn't a trade secret if it is generally known).

Proprietary information includes some trade secrets (such as a secret recipe), but also other information that is neither confidential nor a trade secret (my website design).

Confidential information includes trade secrets. Some confidential information may be proprietary (the secret recipe) but other types may not be (there's a surprise party next week).

Confidential Information Definitions

This contract tip is about defining confidential information (CI).

You can broaden or narrow the definition depending on your client's situation.

Some prefer a broader definition if they expect to share a lot of CI and want protection. They may feel confident that they can protect any received CI from disclosure.

Other companies may want a narrower definition, usually because they receive a lot of valuable trade secrets from others. Another reason is out of concern for later claims that it used the received CI in their products.

A narrow definition might look like this: "labeled as confidential or, if disclosed orally, identified as confidential in writing within 48 hours." This approach is narrow because most companies do not reliably label all their CI and almost no one sends those confirming emails.

A broad CI definition would be: "any information received from a party or its representatives that is not excluded in [the exclusion section]." This approach is so broad that there is a risk it is not be precise enough to create a binding obligation.

I prefer the middle ground: "any information that a reasonable person would understand to be confidential because it is identified as confidential or the circumstances of disclosure."

NDA Landmines

This contract tip is about landmine provisions in non-disclosure agreements (NDAs).

NDAs are important but have risks of their own. The risks increase when the NDAs include unusual provisions that expose a party to greater liability or limit its remedies.

To be clear, these provisions may be appropriate in a corporate merger, employment, or other deals. But they do not belong in typical commercial NDAs.

1. Liquidated damages for breach: Breaches of NDAs are often factually complex. LDs are for objective breaches (like late delivery).

2. Non-Solicitation: It is premature to agree to this provision in an NDA. The parties are just starting to talk.

3. Limitation of Liability: These are very risky. They give the counterparty a price tag for taking and using the other's information.

4. Intellectual Property License or Assignment: Mixing NDAs and licensing terms is not a good idea. If you need a license, sign a more robust agreement with the full scope of terms.

5. Anti-Circumvention: These obligations do not belong in a typical NDA. If it's truly a strategic relationship, include as part of the full agreement.

Indemnification in NDAs

This contract tip is about indemnification in non-disclosure agreements (NDAs).

Smart lawyers have different views on it. But this smart lawyer's view is that commercial NDAs should never include indemnity provisions.

Let me start by saying I think indemnification makes sense in most commercial contracts.

Those agreements include a complex set of rights and obligations to make, deliver, and use a product or service. They include a substantial exchange of value and robust terms around liability and risk.

Not so in an NDA. An NDA just says don't use or disclose my confidential stuff. The parties are just starting to talk. There is no economic exchange. The interaction and relationship are minimal.

I believe indemnification is an inappropriate shifting of risk in this context.

The burden of indemnification is a steep one - paying all costs and often leading the defense of the case. Yet we'd require the other party to an NDA to take all this on before any value exchange because of an allegation around its use or disclosure of information.

The wronged party has a remedy. It can sue for damages and collect, but only after it proves its case. That seems a lot fairer to me in this context.

Warranties in NDAs

This contract tip is about warranties in commercial non-disclosure agreements (NDAs).

The most common is the accuracy disclaimer. It says that the discloser does not warrant that the information is accurate or complete and prohibits the recipient from relying on it.

It is rarely an issue for anyone.

I'm also ok with a warranty that the discloser has the right to share the information it discloses to the recipient. This language gives the recipient a clear claim for breach of contract if the discloser shares something that breach its contract with a third party or infringes a third party's IP.

I sometimes see pushback, but most of the time counterparties approve.

Those two are the only warranty provisions in some NDAs. But when the relationship includes complex technology or data exchange, I may include a warranty compliance with applicable laws. The concept is intended to capture the complex web of privacy, export, and other restrictions on data sharing.

But that's usually it. I generally prefer to keep the warranties very limited due to the limited relationship. More detailed and robust warranties should go in the main agreement.

After You Sign an NDA

This contract tip is about what happens after you sign a non-disclosure agreement (NDA).

If you sign NDAs and file them away thinking you are protected, you may have some surprises.

An NDA is a contract that protects your information and permits you to use the counterparty's information in a limited way BUT ONLY if you do what the NDA requires you to do.

Do you know what is in your NDAs?

Do you know whether you must send a written notice after each meeting confirming the information is confidential?

Do you know what restrictions apply to sharing the counterparty's information with your advisors and contractors?

Do you really want to share your most valuable trade secrets if your NDA allows the counterparty to use and disclose that trade secret after a year?

Get to know your NDAs.

Keep them close.

Do what they say.

Taking those extra steps to understand and comply with your NDAs will go a long way toward protecting your business's trade secrets and confidential information.

Protecting Confidential Information

This contract tip is about protecting confidential information.

Most lawyers and businesspeople know that trade secret law protects some business information. They also know that non-disclosure agreements (NDAs) and confidentiality provisions in other contracts also protect information. Where people get confused is the relationship between the two.

I find the best way to understand the relationship of trade secrets and confidentiality provisions is as a Venn diagram.

Trade secret law protects information that is not generally known, has economic value because it is secret, and the business takes reasonable steps to keep secret. This protection applies even if there is a contract.

Confidentiality provisions in an NDA or other type of contract only protect information to the extent specified in the provision. Whether the information is or is not a trade secret doesn't matter for purposes of the contractual provision.

These two categories sometimes include the same information but sometimes they don't. Combined, trade secret law and confidentiality obligations offer businesses a great way to protect their information.

Three-Party NDAs

This contract tip is about three-party non-disclosure agreements (NDAs).

These work only if precisely drafted to address the complexities. If you are just adding another signature block to your standard two-party NDA, you may have problems down the road. Here's why.

You must clarify how disclosures and liability flow between the parties. For example, can A share the information it receives from B with C? What if C then breaches? Because A shared with C, would we treat C as A's authorized recipient, making A liable?

What about termination? Most three-party NDAs I've seen have the same termination language as two-party NDAs. If so, what happens then if A terminates for convenience? Does the whole NDA go away? Or what if A breaches? Can B immediately terminate the NDA even if C does not agree?

You can draft the NDA provisions to provide clear answers to these situations but that is exactly my point. You have to make sure that you have wording in the three-party NDA to address the different scenarios that flow from having three parties.

For these and many other reasons, I prefer to stick to two-party NDAs. They keep relationships clearer and make it easier to manage the information flow.

CHAPTER 5

CONTRACT STRUCTURE AND FORMATION

Explanation of Master Agreements

This contract tip explains master agreements.

We use the label "master" for contracts that establish a set of terms to govern several transactions between the parties. Think of a master agreement like a bucket. Everything the parties do together goes into that bucket. There are lots of different kinds of master agreements, including master supply agreements, master services agreements, and master license agreements.

You can make any type of contract into a master. To be a master, the agreement must provide that it governs the parties' individual transactions.

Master agreements also include:

- a statement that the master agreement and all the transaction documents are a single unified agreement,

- a process for how the transactions take place (such as purchase orders procedures),

- how the individual transactions relate to the main agreement, including when there are conflicts between them, and

- other terms about big picture concepts that apply to each individual transaction and all as a whole.

The commercial specifics for each transaction (how many, what features, delivery timing) are in the individual ordering documents.

Basics of Contractual Privity

This contract tip is about contractual privity, the principle that a contract only binds the parties to it.

For some reason that I do not understand, many contracts identify a party to a contract as "XYZ Corp. and its affiliates." Ok, so each affiliate is a party too. But when I flip back to the signature page, only XYZ Corp. is signing. There are no signature blocks for the affiliates.

How can the affiliates be parties to a contract when they don't sign or agree to the terms? Short answer? They can't.

To do this properly, consider what you need.

Do the affiliates need to be parties? If yes, then name them and have them sign. If that is too much of a pain, then XYZ Corp. should represent that it has the authority as their agent and sign on their behalf.

If the affiliates need the rights but not the obligations, then identify them as third-party beneficiaries and the scope of their rights.

If the affiliates perform obligations but have no rights, then identify them as subcontractors, any limits on the delegation, and that XYZ Corp. is liable for their acts.

But PLEASE do not just identify affiliates as parties in the first paragraph. It creates confusion. Contracts should create clarity.

Deal Structure for Several Transactions

This contract tip explores fundamental structure issues when parties do several transactions.

If a seller and buyer plan a single transaction, the contract isn't that hard. Seller sells X, buyer pays Y, add the boilerplate. Done!

But when the seller and buyer expect to do several transactions, they must decide whether they should do the transactions under a single contract or enter several contracts? With both structures, the parties can draft the liability caps, the priority of the documents, cross-defaults, licenses, and other terms however they want.

The biggest impact that they cannot draft around is what happens in bankruptcy. In the U.S., our bankruptcy laws provide that bankrupt debtors can assume or reject individual contracts. If you have a single contract with a counterparty and it files for bankruptcy, the counterparty will have to assume or reject all the transactions together. But if you have several contracts, the debtor can cherry-pick, rejecting individual contracts and assuming others.

There is no right or wrong answer. Take the time to figure out which scenario you will want for your transactions if your counterparty becomes bankrupt.

CHAPTER 6

DAMAGES

Sellers' Arguments When Negotiating Limits of Liability

This contract tip is about common arguments used by sellers when negotiating limits of liability.

Sellers have a tough lot. They sell their product for a competitive market price. They need to keep costs low to make a profit. After all, that's why they are in business. But they face potential liability at every turn.

Typical sellers want to limit that liability in their contracts as much as possible to preserve their profit margins and stay in business.

Here are some common arguments sellers make during negotiations:

- I'm not getting paid enough to take on all the risk for this deal.

- My profit margin is not enough to justify this kind of exposure.

- I have risk with my suppliers. I can't take on the buyer's risk too.

- High limits in the contract will encourage the buyer to sue me if anything goes wrong.

- Business is risky. The buyer has to take on some risks of the deal.

Variable Damages in Maximum Liability Provisions

This contract tip looks at the component parts of variable damages in maximum liability provisions.

Most maximum liability provisions include a variable measurement. This approach requires the parties to use objective metrics to calculate the specific amount of the cap. Here are the three main types of metrics that we include. Which we include depends on whether we want to expand or reduce the cap.

1. Value. This metric looks at an underlying financial value. Usually this metric includes at least the amount paid, but sometimes also includes the amount payable too. If we use the amount payable, we need to make sure the parties have a way to measure that amount. It can be tricky when there is no fixed quantity.

2. Product. The metric looks at the category of items to which we apply that value. This metric ranges from an individual product to a category of products to all products. Although often overlooked, this metric is critical in contracts covering multiple goods and services.

3. Applicable Document. This metric looks at the documents used to identify the value and product. It may be a single purchase order, purchase orders over time, the entire agreement, or all agreements between the parties.

How We Label the Limit of Liability Provisions

This contract tip is about how we label the limit of liability provisions.

I have a bad habit of calling them "the consequential damages waiver and the direct damages cap." There are a lot of others who do this too. We need to stop. The problem is we intend for the "direct damages cap" to limit all liability not specifically excluded from this cap. So why do we keep labeling the cap with just one type of liability?

Remember there are three big buckets of liability associated with a contract - direct damages, indirect or consequential damages, and other liability that isn't a damage. This last category includes indemnification and some warranty claims.

You may think "We only need it to cap direct damages. We already waived all consequential damages." Let's look at that. Usually there are exceptions to that waiver. Should you cap the excluded indirect damages? What about the other non-damage liability? If you aren't specific about it, a court, jury, or arbitrator may read it differently than you intended.

Limits of liability are one of the most important provisions and a pivotal concept in many contract disputes. Join me in trying to break this bad habit. Stop calling it a direct damages cap.

Watch Out for Liquidated Damages with No End Date

This contract tip is to watch out for liquidated damages provisions (LDs) that have no end date.

LDs are complicated beasts that require drafting precision. Most contracts get the basics right and include the required language. Yeah for lawyers!

But what they often leave out is what happens when the triggering event goes on indefinitely. A typical LD says that if the seller does not deliver by the due date, the seller will pay 1% of the price per week of delay, up to 8% maximum.

Sounds fine, right? Not for a buyer still waiting for delivery at week 10, week 20, or later. The buyer agreed that the LDs are the exclusive remedy, so the buyer may be stuck with that remedy no matter how long the delay or the impact on its business.

Sure, smart litigators could make arguments, but they'd struggle to get around that exclusive remedy. I was involved in a case like this in which our recovery for nine months of delay on a critical piece of equipment was the 10% LD cap.

I learned my lesson. Since then, when I represent buyers, I always draft LDs as an exclusive remedy only for the first X days of delivery delay. I then identify the buyer's other rights if the delivery has not occurred by the time we reach the maximum LD cap.

Setting the Maximum Liability in a B2B Commercial Contract

This contract tip is about setting the maximum liability in a B2B commercial contract.

I wish I had an easy rule to give you. Industry standards provide a starting point, but I encourage you not to stop there. Always do the analysis to make sure the provision works for your deal.

Here's the four-part framework I use:

1. I evaluate whether we are more or less likely to cause damages that may occur under this agreement. It can depend on things like the seller's scope, the buyer's involvement in the design, and how the end customer will use the product.

2. I consider the proportionality of potential damages. Are we both going to suffer greatly if something goes wrong or will one side bear the brunt?

3. I look at risk factors. What are the performance requirements, the potential for third party claims, creditworthiness, and reputation of the counterparty, and risks with these goods?

4. I think about risk mitigation. Is this cap within our insurance? Are there exceptions to the cap? Can we shift liability to a third party? Do we have systems in place to mitigate the risk ourselves?

Think through the real-world risk and exposure first. Then ensure your maximum liability provision aligns with them.

What are Incidental Damages

This contract tip is about incidental damages.

Incidental damages are costs and expenses that a party incurs while mitigating and dealing with the breach by the other party.

Incidental damages include things like warehouse storage costs for sellers when their buyers improperly reject goods and for buyers when sellers deliver the wrong goods.

The Uniform Commercial Code (UCC) in the U.S. allows both sellers and buyers to collect incidental damages if they are reasonable. (UCC 2-215(1) and 2-210)

What perplexes me is that most sale of goods contracts I read have both parties waiving their rights to incidental damages as part of the section that waives consequential damages. But why? I don't get it. It seems reasonable to me that sellers and buyers should get reimbursed for their incidental damages.

I understand that the parties may want to include incidental damages as part of an overall cap on damages, but I don't understand why incidentals are often waived.

Options for Setting Limits of Liability

This contract tip is about the options for setting limits of liability.

The choice is not binary. There is a continuum of provisions that increase or decrease a party's risk. You can choose a provision that provides almost no liability for a party, one that has unlimited liability for a party, or the many variations in between.

Here's a continuum of possible approaches from the highest to the lowest risk for a seller.

- No provision limiting seller's liability.

- Seller's liability limited for a narrow set of claims, unlimited for the rest.

- Seller's liability limited to the value of all agreements between the seller and its affiliates with the buyer and its affiliates.

- Seller's liability limited to the value of all agreements between seller and buyer.

- Seller's liability limited to the greater of $X or the value of the agreement.

- Seller's liability limited to the value of the agreement.

- Seller's liability limited to the value of the agreement for X months.

- Seller's liability limited to the smallest transaction document (usually a statement of work or purchase order).

CHAPTER 7

DEFINITIONS

Definitions in Contracts

This contract tip is about contract definitions.

I consider the decision on where to place definitions to be a stylistic one. I just make sure each capitalized term is defined and only defined once. What is not stylistic is including rights and obligations in a definition. That is just wrong.

Here's why. Definitions are shortcuts in a contract. Rather than type a detailed concept each time, we use a single defined term. It's an awesome technique and makes contracts so much easier to read. But the mechanism breaks down when you include rights and obligations in the definition.

Here is the right and wrong way to write a contract definition:

- CORRECT: "Site means the Buyer's warehouse at 123 Main Street, Austin, Texas."

- INCORRECT: "Site means the Buyer's warehouse at 123 Main Street, Austin, Texas. Buyer will store the Product in a secured area in the Site."

If you use the incorrect version, every time the word Site appears in the contract, you will need to read it as the full definition. That means you would repeat the obligation about storage every single time.

You would never repeat the same sentence 20 times in a contract. But that is exactly what including an obligation in a definition does. So, don't do that.

Nuances of Drafting Definitions

This contract tip is to about the nuances of drafting definitions.

Watch your definitions carefully. Definitions are one of the most important AND most overlooked parts of a contract. There are lots of subtle techniques for drafting definitions in ways to limit liability.

Here is a common example. A seller's form contract defines "Product" as a specific piece of equipment identified in the product datasheet and assigned this product number. Sounds fine, right? Maybe. But not if the seller is providing ancillary items like connectors or spare parts that the buyer assumes are included in the warranty and other contract terms.

Check to see what the seller's warranty and indemnification covers. Often in these cases, these and other clauses will only cover the Products. By narrowing the definition to include less than all of what the seller sold to the buyer, the seller narrows its liability and obligations.

Watch out for this technique when purchasing goods or services. Make sure the Product (or whatever term you use) includes everything bought under a purchase order from the seller. Otherwise, you may be surprised when you try to make a claim. Only then will you discover that your purchase is not protected under the contract.

Aligning Defined Terms with Statutory Definitions

This contract tip is about defining terms in your contracts already defined by the applicable statutes.

Do not add your own version of statutory terms to your contracts. Let me explain why this is such a bad idea.

Not long ago, I reviewed a counterparty's form of non-disclosure agreement governed by California law. The counterparty had added its own original definition of a trade secret. I checked and it is worded differently from the California statutory definition.

This has disaster written all over it. Let's say I left that provision in and there was a dispute over a party's disclosure of the other party's trade secrets. What definition of trade secret would a court or arbitrator use in evaluating the case? The version defined in the contract or the version that would apply under California law? A combination of both?

Your guess is as good as mine. Redefining statutory terms creates confusion in your contracts. Let the statute's definition control. If you want to clarify that approach in the contract, define the term as the meaning under applicable law.

CHAPTER 8

DISPUTES AND DISPUTE RESOLUTION

Required Negotiation Periods

This contract tip is about including a required negotiation period BEFORE filing for litigation, arbitration, or mediation.

These provisions usually say that if there is a dispute, the senior executives must meet during a set period to resolve it. Neither party may file for litigation or arbitration until that period is complete.

This approach may seem like a good idea. What could be bad about negotiating before taking more drastic steps? I was trained long ago to delete these and still do when I can.

Here's why.

- What if my client has a strategic need to sue ASAP? This need could be to get equitable relief or secure a preferred forum. Why reduce the client's options?

- What if my client is using litigation as part of a business strategy? This need happens sometimes, and in these cases there is no interest in resolving the issue.

- If not 1 or 2, you can bet that the parties already tried hard to work it out and failed. Litigation and arbitration are their last resort. Why impose another discussion period on top of what they've already done?

Complying with Contracts During an Ongoing Dispute

This contract tip is about complying with contracts during an ongoing dispute.

"Always wear the white hat." That was the advice I learned as a young lawyer. In old movies, the cowboy with the white hat was the good guy. The one with the black hat was usually dastardlier.

When in a dispute, we want the judge, jury, or arbitrator to perceive our client as the good one, an innocent victim of the other side's mistakes and bad acts.

What does this mean in practice? No nasty emails. Pay undisputed fees. Be ready to perform required tasks. Hold up their side of the bargain.

This advice may not apply to every situation. Each case needs to be assessed, which may lead to a different approach.

But without other advice, I tell my clients not to start acting badly or blatantly breaching the agreement just because there is a dispute, and they think the other breached first.

The reason? What if your client stops performing, relying on the other side's prior breach, but the decision maker disagrees and does not think the counterparty breached first? When they look at the timeline, they may think your client was the one who breached first, giving the counterparty a right to damages.

Play it safe and be nice.

Choice of Litigation Venue for Two U.S. Parties

This contract tip is about choice of venue when two U.S. parties want litigation to resolve disputes. I expect aspects apply to other countries too.

Consider these five things as you decide:

1. Does the jurisdiction allow you to select it for this deal? Some states are open (California), some have a handful of limitations (New York), and others states flat out do not allow venue unless a party has a connection. So make sure you can select the jurisdiction before you do.

2. Do you have a "suing the Pope in Vatican City" problem? If your counterpart is the largest employer in a particular county, it may not be a good idea to have the litigation there.

3. Where are the records and people? If everyone and everything related to the engagement is in Seattle, does it really make sense to sue in Maine?

4. Can you afford to manage complex litigation across the country? The less legal budget you have, the more painful a faraway lawsuit may be.

5. Do you need to specify venue? If you don't agree on where, especially in small contracts, the solution is sometimes to just delete it. Another option I always liked is to place venue in the defendant's hometown. It discourages running to the courthouse to file first.

Resolving Contract Disputes in The Real World

This contract tip is about resolving contract disputes in the real world.

Some law students might believe that when there are commercial contract disputes, the businesses file for arbitration or litigation as specified in the contract. In my experience, that rarely happens.

Almost all businesses will bend over backward - even accept some undeserved losses - to resolve disputes through informal negotiations.

So even when the parties are in a dispute over a contract, it is still improbable that an arbitrator or judge will ever read that contract.

It is much more likely that the most critical people to ever read your disputed contract will be the senior executives for both parties. These executives will review the document with their lawyers and explore if it includes a path to resolution.

While I prepare contracts in case of litigation (of course), I don't think of the judges and arbitrators as the primary audience for my contracts that may end up in a dispute.

I write my contracts more for the future business executives looking at it for a way out of a future crisis.

Chapter 9

DRAFTING

How to Handle Making a Mistake in a Contract

This contract tip is how to handle making a mistake in a contract.

It has happened to all of us. If it hasn't happened to you yet, it will. Here are three tips for dealing with your contract mistakes:

Take a breath. Discovering your own mistakes can be overwhelming and anxiety-inducing. You'll need to think rationally and that is hard to do when you are emotional. So wait until you calm down to evaluate next steps.

After taking that breath (and not much after), tell someone.

If you are the junior person on a team, let your manager or team lead know what happened. The absolute worst thing you can do as a junior attorney is trying to cover it up.

Senior members of your team have more experience dealing with these things. They will give you a path forward.

If you are working on the deal by yourself, evaluate the mistake's impact and your options.

If the contract hasn't been signed, you still have time to change it. Introducing the change may irritate the other side, but it happens. It usually works out fine.

If the mistake is in the signed contract, consider whether it is worth asking for the amendment. Your counterparty may value the relationship over that term and agree to it.

If not, try to mitigate and then move on.

Perennial Legal Debate of Whether to Use Will or Shall

This contract tip is about the perennial legal debate of whether to use will or shall.

Much blood has been shed... Uh, well, ok, not really.

But a lot of people get very worked up about whether to use will or shall in contracts.

Me? I'm agnostic on the whole thing. Maybe I'm more apathetic. I like will better but was trained to use shall. I try at least to be consistent, but I'm sure both end up in the same contract sometimes. There may be some passionate academics and militant grammarians who are aghast that I am not following whatever "rule" they adopted.

The absolute truth is that no one wants me to spend time proofreading each use of will and shall. My clients (like yours I expect) want me to be practical and focus on where they face a real risk.

There are a million things that could go wrong with my commercial deals. I spend my time on the issues that matter, like payment, warranties, intellectual property, indemnification, and limits of liability. The likelihood that the use of will or shall determines anything in my contracts is so small it is close to zero.

Ignore the will/shall debate. Focus on more meaningful concepts in the scarce time you have for contract review.

How Not to Amend Contracts

This contract tip is about how not to amend contracts.

Avoid amending prior contracts in other random contracts between the parties. Instead, amend contracts in a stand-alone separate document called an amendment. Label each amendment with its sequential number.

I was reminded of the importance of this practice when I recently reviewed a services agreement with a provision like this: "This amendment relates to the part of the [prior agreement] with the payment process."

It then described the change generally, but with no reference to the section or exact words that were being changed.

What a mess.

Imagine you are the lawyer dealing with a dispute about the prior agreement. How in the world would you know that a random latter contract amended the terms?

Even if you did know, this vague amendment would make it hard to figure out exactly what changed. Don't take this approach.

Prepare amendments as stand-alone documents that do nothing other than amending or adding new terms to that agreement. Label each amendment with the sequential number to help everyone track all the changes and the order in which they were made.

Amending contracts this way makes life easier for everyone.

Cutting and Pasting to Create Contracts

This contract tip is about cutting and pasting to create contracts.

Cutting and pasting involves taking language from a sample contract and pasting it into another. I've heard some call it a negative thing.

I disagree. I think it is a wonderful technique that serves us well. There is a reason why lawyers cut and paste from other contracts. It is not because we are lazy. It is not because we are unskilled. It is because it works.

Yes, there are tools out there that try to automate parts of this process. But most require a considerable investment of time and money that we don't have. Even if we use them, they do not have everything we need.

So when we need to add a new provision, we look online or search our contract files for the right sample language. And then we cut and paste.

Of course, cutting and pasting can never be the end. We always must edit, customize, improve, and fix the existing language.

But that is precisely our job, isn't it? We revise provisions to customize for the context, the terminology, the deal, and the client. After all, fixing contract language is a lawyer's superpower. 👌 ✏️ 🗒️

Stand tall and stand proud, fellow lawyers. We are the cut and pasters.

Drafting Contracts to Follow the Logical Order of Events

This contract tip is about drafting contracts to follow the logical order of events.

Contracts are easier to read when we present concepts in the order that readers expect. Most commercial contracts are set up in this general order - general obligations (such as delivery and inspection), then payment, then warranty and remedies, then termination, then indemnification, then the other boilerplate.

If I see the payment terms in the boilerplate or a general delivery obligation after the warranty, it throws me off. It makes the whole contract harder to digest.

The same approach applies to provisions that describe events occurring over time. I organize them following the timeline.

For the purchase of goods, I organize the sections as purchase process, shipment, delivery, inspection, payment, warranty, remedies. That order is how they usually occur in the real world.

I also apply this sequential approach within individual provisions. I don't describe the third step followed by the second and then the first. I write the provision, so the sentences follow the order that the events occur.

Our brains prefer to process things logically and sequentially. Write contracts the way our brains work.

Say Everything in A Contract Only Once

This contract tip is to say everything in a contract only once.

One of the first contracts I reviewed as a new attorney was for a franchisor client that wanted to terminate a contract. I was supposed to write up an explanation of its rights in the agreement. I still remember finding three provisions on the subject, each describing its rights in a different way.

I was clueless. Which of those was the right one? Which one could our client rely on?

The only real answer? Who the hell knows?

Sure, we can argue about the parties' meeting of the mind, come up with an interpretation that explains how the three provisions could be read together, or generally reach deep into the lawyer treasure trove for other clever arguments.

But the real problem was that we had no idea which argument would fly. The client was left guessing on something that should have been clear.

Now, 25 years later, I'm still reading contracts with the same problems. I read an NDA this week that restated a concept eight (yes, I counted) different and conflicting ways scattered throughout a three-page agreement.

Do not do that. Address each concept once. Save yourself and your clients the headaches of trying to figure out the repetitiveness.

Correctly Identifying Names in Your Contracts

This contract tip is about correctly identifying names in your contracts.

I'm not talking about the names of the parties, although to clarify, yes, you should get those right too.

I'm talking about all the other names that appear - entities, rules, statutes, regulations, government agencies, and people.

It is alarming how often they are incorrect. For example, if you designate a particular arbitration entity, get the spelling right. (Hint – It is the Hong Kong International Arbitration Centre, not Center.)

While you are checking the name of the entity, confirm the name of the rules. Most arbitration bodies have different rules available for different disputes and parties. So, don't say just "JAMS arbitration rules." Say, "JAMS Engineering and Construction Arbitration Rules & Procedures for Expedited Arbitration" or whichever rules you designate.

I verify every name and reference in my contracts during my final proofread before execution. I recommend you do that too.

Accurate names = clearer contracts = happiness for lawyers.

How to Pick a Starting Template for a New or Complex Deal

This contract drafting tip is about how to pick a starting template for a new or complex deal.

Most companies have standard templates. The problem is when you have a new type or more complex transaction that requires a different form. Which template should you pick as a starting point?

When the answer is not obvious, I start by mapping out key concepts. Being clear on the four items below helps me narrow it down.

1. Product design – Which party does what to create the product? Is it standard off the shelf or a mix of seller and buyer input?

2. Creation – Who will create or manufacture the product and what is its relationship to your counterparty? If the vendor is selling third-party products, is it your counterparty or the original creator/manufacturer standing behind the quality and dealing with problems?

3. Delivery and risk of loss – Where and how will delivery take place? For physical goods, what Incoterm will apply and when does title pass?

4. End use – What rights in the product do the end users need? Who will use the product and make warranty claims? What do we expect the vendor to do if the product breaks down?

5. Thinking through these things usually gives me enough information to pick the right starting template.

Reviewing the Specifications and Scope of Work

This contract tip is about reviewing the specifications and scope of work attached to a purchase order (PO) or contract.

Specifications describe all the features and requirements for the goods purchased. A scope of work describes the tasks, deliverables, and other requirements for the services performed.

Even though these documents are usually prepared by the technical and business teams, a lawyer or experienced contract professional needs to review every word. Every word. I don't review them to provide substantive input.

I review them for three reasons:

1. Make sure it makes sense - I must be able to generally understand the concepts described. Because if I can't, how is a jury or arbitrator going to?

2. Make sure no concepts overlap with or belong in the main body of the contract or PO - I find duplicative provisions about 50% of the time. I also sometimes catch the other side trying to sneak in substantive contract terms like warranty limitations by adding to the specifications

3. Make sure the writing is clear - Technical and businesspeople often write in passive tense. And passive tense is a big no-no in contracts.

Always read your specifications and scopes of work.

Chapter 10

GOVERNING LAW

Excluding Choice of Law Rules

This contract tip is about excluding choice of law rules in your contract's governing law provision.

A typical choice of law provisions reads "All matters arising from or relating to this Agreement are governed by the laws of California without regard to its choice of law rules." Many people include this language about choice of law rules without really understanding why it is in there and what it means.

The reason we ALWAYS include this phrase is what happens if you don't. It goes back to civil procedure and the rules that jurisdictions must decide what their laws apply when a dispute relates to more than one jurisdiction.

The law on this issue is called "Conflicts of Law." Each jurisdiction has rules for what law applies when.

One problem that can occur is an endless loop called renvoi. Renvoi happens when a jurisdiction's choice of law rules designate that the laws of a different jurisdiction apply. But when you go to apply that different jurisdiction's laws, they point you back to the first jurisdiction. What a mess.

We don't like anything super complicated or messy in contracts. We like simple and clear. Keep your contract's governing law clear by excluding the conflict of law rules.

Governing Law Provisions in International Sale of Goods Contracts

This contract tip is about governing law provisions in international sale of goods contracts. The governing law provisions must always exclude the U.N. Convention on Contracts for the International Sale of Goods (CISG).

If you aren't familiar with it, CISG is a U.N. convention that establishes default rules for cross-border commercial contracts, much like the way the Uniform Commercial Code (UCC) does in the U.S. There are 96 countries have signed CISG, including the U.S., Canada, Mexico, Australia, China, and Russia.

While I appreciate that CISG exists, it is a gap filler and not needed in contracts governed by U.S. law. We cover all the essential concepts in the contract or indirectly through the UCC.

What some do not know is that CISG's default provisions AUTOMATICALLY apply to ALL contracts for the sale of goods between parties from different signatory countries. The ONLY way to have CISG not apply to these contracts is to add an exclusion and say it does not apply.

While the CISG exclusion is needed only if both parties are from signatory countries, I typically include it in all my international contracts for the sale of goods. If a party later assigns the contract, the exclusion is already there.

CHAPTER 11

INDEMNIFICATION

Basics of Indemnification

This contract tip explains the basics of indemnification.

Indemnification is a legal way to say reimbursement. We include these provisions to establish the reimbursement requirements if one of the parties is responsible for damages to the other party or its cohorts.

A lot of people get overwhelmed by indemnification provisions. They are very hard to digest and read. It doesn't help that most contracts have the core elements as one very long sentence. I've found the best way to review an indemnity is to break it down into its elements and then consider each part on its own.

Here are the nine questions to ask to identify each element of an indemnification provision:

1. Who is indemnifying?

2. Who is being indemnified?

3. Is there a defense obligation too?

4. What kinds of damages are covered?

5. What relationship is required between the damages and the underlying events?

6. What types of underlying events are covered?

7. Are there any exclusions?

8. Is indemnification the sole remedy for the underlying event?

9. What indemnification process is required?

Nuances Around the Indemnified Parties

This contract tip is about a drafting technique used to deflect the focus off the number of indemnified parties.

To deemphasize the entities and people included as indemnified parties, define "Indemnified Parties" in the definition section instead of in the provision. This technique exploits our rush to review and how hard it is to track contract definitions out of context.

When we read a section and see a term is defined elsewhere, we either:

- immediately find the definition, read for understanding, go back to the provision to see the context, and make any changes to the definition; or

- we take a quick unconscious guess at what the definition says and keep reading, with the intent to look at it closely later.

The problem? Later sometimes doesn't come. There are 100+ details to watch for in the shorter contracts, 1000+ in the bigger ones. When the section does not include the list of indemnified parties, lawyers often overlook it during later reviews.

My advice? When you read indemnification for the first time, either review it in-depth at that moment or add a note to check the indemnified party later. Be careful that you don't skim through and then forget about it.

How to Draft Indemnified Party Language

This contract tip includes how to draft the indemnified party language in an indemnification provision.

Indemnification provisions identify who must reimburse whom when covered events cause damages. There are a lot of choices about who to include as an indemnified party. This is another concept that has no right or wrong answer.

What language you use will depend on your risks and bargaining power. Here is a ranking of possible indemnified parties with the seller indemnifying, ranked from the seller's smallest indemnification obligation to its biggest.

- No indemnity provision

- "Seller indemnifies Buyer"

- "Seller indemnifies Buyer and its directors and officers"

- "Seller indemnifies Buyer and its directors, officers, and employees"

- "Seller indemnifies Buyer and its directors, officers, employees, and agents"

- "Seller indemnifies Buyer and its directors, officers, employees, agents, contractors, representatives, and customers"

- "Seller indemnifies Buyer and its Affiliates, and their respective directors, officers, employees, agents, contractors, representatives, and customers"

The more entities and people in the indemnified party list, the riskier it is for the party indemnifying.

Who Should Be an Indemnified Party

This contract tip is about indemnified parties.

Indemnification provisions identify who receives reimbursement for the specified damages and claims. The one who must pay is called the indemnifying party. Those who receive reimbursement are indemnified parties.

Who should be as included as indemnified parties? The answer depends on your risks and bargaining power.

Here's is a three-part process to figure it out.

1. Is the indemnification mutual or one-way? If the provision is one-way, use the indemnified party language that most favors your client. Be careful, though. You may have to make the provision mutual during negotiations. If that could happen, draft the indemnified party language with a more even-handed approach.

2. Which party is more at risk for causing damages and claims for the covered events? If you are more likely to cause the damages, then you are more likely to be reimbursing. In that case, keep indemnified parties' scope to a limited number. If you expect the opposite, expand to add more indemnified parties.

3. What related entities and people also may be subject to claims? Consider the obligations in the contract. If your affiliates and contractors are heavily involved, push to include them too.

CHAPTER 12

INTELLECTUAL PROPERTY

Intangible Nature of Intellectual Property

This contract tip is about the intangible nature of intellectual property (IP).

Everyone who works on contracts with IP provisions needs to understand how IP works. One of the hardest things to get our heads around is that the property rights are intangible. IP owners have rights to something that has no physical properties. It isn't like property rights to land, where you can pick up a clump of dirt and say, "I own this." It isn't like owning a car or a house, where you can see and touch what you own.

With IP, you just own rights. Even if we understand that concept, it is easy to get confused when we think about works protected by IP - a patent for a machine that filters water, a copyright in a painting hanging on the wall, or a trademark logo on a cup of coffee.

"But those are all tangible things that you can touch." Yes, very true. But those are physical embodiments of the IP. Those objects are not the IP itself. The IP owners own rights to do certain acts relating to that machine, that painting, or that logo. But the IP owner does not own each physical embodiment of those rights.

It's kind of like Schrodinger's cat. "It is both tangible property and intangible property at the same time."

Core Elements of an Intellectual Property License

This contract tip is about the core elements of an intellectual property license provision.

Most contracts have license provisions as one long convoluted sentence. They are full of complex concepts, making it difficult to process.

The best way for me to understand these provisions is to break them down into parts. I look for answers to these nine questions in every license provision:

- Who is granting the license?
- Who is granted the license?
- Is the license exclusive?
- Does the licensee have to pay anything?
- Can the licensee transfer or sublicense its rights?
- How long is the license and can it be canceled?
- Where can the licensee exercise its rights?
- What specific rights are granted to the licensee?
- What intellectual property is being licensed?

There are of course lots of other elements to consider adding to your license provision depending on the situation. You also may see individual parts in standalone sections, as they need more detail to describe the scope.

As a licensee, make sure that you can use the licensed intellectual property in the ways that you need to use it. As a licensor, check that you are not granting broader rights to the licensee than is necessary for the deal.

Using the Correct Words in a Copyright License

This contract tip is about using the correct words in a copyright license provision.

Most contract drafting is flexible. We can write provisions in a lot of different ways if we precisely capture the concept. Not so with the copyright license grant. Copyrights are created by statutes. The only rights that exist under copyright law are the ones laid out in those statutes.

Section 106 of the U.S. Copyright Act provides that the owner of a copyright has an exclusive right to do and authorize others to do just five things with the work:

- reproduce,
- prepare derivative works,
- distribute,
- display, and
- perform.

Those five rights are the only rights that a U.S. copyright owner has and can license.

It is ok to include other words in the license grant. We sometimes add them when we want to precisely capture some other concept. The most common non-copyright word I see is "use." Just remember that these non-copyright words should never be the only rights in the grant provision.

Always include the exact words from the copyright statute in your copyright license grant.

Who Grants the License in a License Provision?

This contract tip is about who grants the license in a license provision.

Who is granting the license seems straightforward.

It can be, but sometimes it gets more complicated. Here are some examples of this clause: ""Seller grants...," "Seller and its Affiliates grant...," or "Seller, on behalf of itself and its Affiliates, grants..."

Check for these four things about the licensors in your contract.

1. Are there representations and warranties about the licensors' authority to grant the license? Make sure the rep and warranty specifically cover all the licensors.

2. Are all the licensors signing the agreement? If not, is there a representation and warranty from the signing party that it has the right to make this grant on behalf of the others?

3. Do the warranty and non-infringement provisions include the licenses granted by all the licensors or just by the signing party?

4. Is the other licensor really doing a direct grant to the licensee in this contract? Sometimes drafters confuse sublicenses. If someone has the right to grant sublicenses, it grants those directly, not on behalf of the original licensor.

Always check the rest of the contract terms to make sure they match who is granting the license.

Who Is Granted A License in A License Provision

This contract tip is about the parties granted a license in a license provision.

The provision is straightforward when there is a single licensee that also signs the agreement. It gets more complicated when the license extends to other entities too. Some examples are "Seller grants to Buyer and its Affiliates..." and "Seller grants to Buyer and its Contract Manufacturer..."

Here are three things to think about:

1. Do the other licensees need a direct license from the Seller? Consider whether Seller is better off giving the Buyer the right to grant sublicenses to specific entities or categories. The Buyer would be responsible for their compliance, but it removes some of Seller's control over those users.

2. How are the other licensees bound by the license terms if not signing the agreement? What document or terms do you have controlling their use? Who will ensure each licensee agrees to it?

3. What happens if the Buyer is sold and ends up with many affiliates? What if one of the new affiliates is a direct competitor? This approach could be problematic if the license or pricing mechanism is not scalable. Consider whether you should include restrictions on competitors' rights to use.

CHAPTER 13

NEGOTIATION

Client's Priorities During Negotiations

This contract tip is about the client's priorities during negotiations.

Always ask yourself why your client is doing this deal.

I know this.

It isn't so you can engage in a battle of wits with the counterparty's lawyer.

It isn't so you can make the contract into a work of art.

It isn't so you can see how many concessions you can extract from the other side.

Your client's goal for the deal is to create a business relationship that allows the parties to pursue an opportunity that benefits them both.

We know this in our heads, but it is easy to get caught up in the negotiation as an end to itself. After all, that is our task and focus. Plus, we lawyers want to win. We are overachievers and trained to be zealous advocates for our clients.

That all leads us to focus on making each provision protect our client as much as possible. While important, we also must temper that with why the client engaged us.

The client hired us to help the business achieve the outcome. That outcome is why the client is negotiating the contract with the counterparty. The contract is only part of what determines the success or failure of that outcome. That outcome always needs to be the priority. In other words, don't win the battles only to lose the war.

Your Own Negotiation Style

This contract tip is about finding our approach to contract negotiations.

The evolution of my negotiation style reminds me of the fairy tale Goldilocks and the Three Bears. You remember - one chair was too soft, one was too hard, and one was just right.

As a new lawyer, I had a lot of fear about negotiations. I knew I'd screw it all up and embarrass myself in front of my client. I was so anxious and that made me less effective. This approach was too soft.

After I had some experience, I became more aggressive. I went into the sessions with my guard up. I might be smiling, but I was ready for battle. Eventually, I realized that didn't work great. I was too quick to argue and too slow to compromise. This approach was too hard.

At some point, I settled into a more conversational approach, which is what I use now.

I talk to my counterparty as I would someone at a social event. I don't yell, I don't insult, and I don't get angry. I try to make it a pleasant conversation, even when we disagree. This approach is just right for me.

My point is that we all evolve in how we approach negotiations.

Watch how others do it.

Explore different techniques.

Continue until you find the style just right for you.

How to Use Communication Channels During Negotiations

This contract tip is about how to use communication channels during negotiations.

My technology deals usually have three or four channels available - legal, technical, business, and, in some strategic negotiations, senior executive.

Typically, the business leads work out the commercial terms first. Then the entire group meets to discuss and agree upon the contract terms.

This approach is often all we need. But sometimes it is not. Sometimes we need to do something more to get to consensus. This need happens when the deal is especially complex or high value, when the parties are not that aligned, or when there is a difficult individual on one of the teams.

In those cases, I consider whether using other communication channels could help.

When the other lawyer seems reasonable, I may propose the two lawyers have a separate call to work out some of the legal wording on already-agreed concepts.

When we are struggling to agree on KPIs or technical details, I might suggest that we ask the technical leads to discuss offline.

And when we reach an impasse on the core commercial or risk terms, we'll have the business leads or senior executives meet separately to see if they can resolve the differences.

Dealing with What You Don't Know

This contract tip is about dealing with what you don't know during negotiations.

It happens to all of us. The other side makes a statement of fact. "Patent exhaustion means that no license is required here" or "The laws in my country do not allow venue in the U.S." Sometimes it is hooey and sometimes it is not.

But at that moment, you don't know which.

As a new lawyer, I'd bluff my way through. I'd do my best not to let on that I didn't know and quickly say, "Let me talk to my client about it offline." I'd then go into deep research mode to figure it out.

Now, rather than pretend that I know, I admit my ignorance and ask the other side to explain it to me. I ask about the big picture and the nuances, what is absolute and what is flexible, and what options there are for dealing with it.

There are lots of reasons why this approach often works better. I've now got them on my side helping me understand and solve for this issue. Chris Voss talked a lot about this approach in his book Never Split the Difference. I love this technique.

It also provides useful clues and intelligence. Even if I don't understand the legal argument, I now understand my counterpart's view of it. And that is always valuable.

Deals on The Terms We Want

This contract tip is about our ability to reach a deal that has the terms we want.

One of the most important mindsets for negotiators is to remember: We are not in control. We can't make the other side agree with us.

We can try of course. That is the entire point of negotiations - to see if there is common ground on which both sides want to do this deal. We use our best drafting and negotiating techniques to influence and persuade. But in the end, we cannot force our counterparties to sign because we are not in control of them.

Now we all get frustrated when they won't agree to the edits we want. Some negotiators get downright angry. They rant about the other side not being "reasonable," which really means the other side does not agree to the ranters' proposals.

In my experience, those ranters do more harm than good. Their uncontrolled emotion ruins the trust and goodwill you need to find consensus and leaves the other side even more reluctant to see things the ranters' way.

I prefer the more serene approach to negotiations. Negotiate to include as many of your changes as possible. When you have the deal as far as you can, then you either sign or you don't. That decision is something of which you are in control.

Efforts Clauses as Negotiating Tools

This tip is about using efforts clauses - reasonable efforts, best efforts, and the like - as valuable tools for contract negotiations.

Many attorneys, myself included, learned that we can adjust an obligation by inserting one of the efforts clauses.

Some academics go into great detail explaining the conflicting case law and that we cannot be certain how a court will interpret the phrase.

I'm ok with that. The value I see is not in its certainty but as a tool for reaching consensus.

Let's say a buyer wants the seller to commit to some task. The seller is reluctant and wants to delete it.

In comes the efforts clause.

The buyer can acknowledge the seller's challenges and offer an efforts clause to soften the obligation. And this approach often works because the seller perceives the obligation is reduced by that efforts clause.

I love this solution - the buyer is happy because it keeps the obligation, and the seller is happy because it reduced the obligation. Now we can get the deal done.

And in the real world getting a deal done has a lot more value for companies than having certainty about an efforts qualifier.

Negotiating with Little Bargaining Power

This contract tip covers negotiating deals when you have little bargaining power.

We've all been there. You receive a one-sided contract from a big company. You may think trying to negotiate is hopeless, but it may not be.

Here are my four best strategies for this situation:

1. Don't make assumptions. You may be surprised by your leverage. If the customer wants your product or a seller needs to hit a quarterly quota, you may see more concessions.

2. Ask nicely. If you are friendly or have some bargaining power, there may be room to negotiate. Most big companies use playbooks with pre-approved changes. Remember the decision to give on these is at the discretion of the attorney. So be nice.

3. Make just a few changes. If you ask for 100 changes, you may only get a few and ones you don't want. Focus on the most important issues and ask for a limited number and be reasonable. This approach makes it much more likely you'll get some.

4. Include something you can give up. In most negotiations, it is unlikely you'll get everything. Ask for at least one point that you can concede. Don't go in needing every change.

And remember the wise words of Commander Taggart - "Never give up. Never surrender!"

Prepping the Document to Send to the Other Side

This contract tip is about prepping the document to send to the other side.

Did you know if you use an existing Word document as the starting point, it may have the source information still embedded and hidden in the document?

If that freaks you out (as it should), then run the "Check for Issues" feature within Word on every document before you send it to the other side. It identifies any metadata, hidden text, or other things you don't want the counterparty to see.

Follow these nine steps:

1. Select "File"
2. Select "Info"
3. Select "Check for Issues"
4. Select "Inspect Documents"
5. Check the boxes of what you want to clear. I usually uncheck "Comments, Revisions, and Versions" and "Headers, Footers, and Watermarks."
6. Click "Inspect" in the dialog box.
7. After it runs, you'll see another box that says, "Review the inspection results." You'll see any identifying properties detected.
8. Clear them by hitting "Remove All."
9. You can reinspect by hitting the "Reinspect" button or just close.

That's it. Just a few steps that may save you from a whole lot of embarrassment.

Exchanging Redlines with a Counterparty

This contract tip is about exchanging redlines with a counterparty.

Redlines or redlined contracts are electronic versions of a contract that show the differences between two versions. All contract negotiations start with a template form. The other party then adds its changes to the form.

The typical practice is to then send a redlined version back to the other party that shows all the changes made to the received version.

Many lawyers will work off that redlined copy received from the other side.

Not me.

I learned early on to ALWAYS run my own redline. When I run my own redline, I often see changes that don't show up as changed in the redline that I received from the counterparty.

I believe in most cases this is unintentional. Running redlines is a very manual effort. Sometimes people choose the wrong base document without realizing it. I have had only a few occasions in my career when I thought the incorrect redline was purposefully deceptive.

Just remember that you cannot control the two documents that your counterparty used to create the redline. But you can control the choice when you do it yourself. Always run your own redlines.

Using Your Negotiating Currency

This contract tip is about using your negotiating currency.

When I was a new attorney, I was very methodical in how I revised contracts. For each provision, I'd make sure I knew what the academics said was the best drafting approach for that concept. Then I'd revise each provision to say that.

I don't do that anymore.

Don't get me wrong. I still consider the academic recommendations for contract drafting. They have spent years studying the case law and provide a ton of value and wisdom.

But now, as an experienced attorney, I focus mainly on how and where I want to spend my negotiating currency.

Negotiating currency is what I call the amount of stuff you can realistically change in a contract for that deal. Each negotiation is different in how much you can change without putting your client's priorities at risk.

The approach I use is to make sure I am fully aware of the real world risks we face if things go wrong. There are common risks (nonpayment and product quality) and less frequent but very dangerous risks (patent infringement).

I focus my energy and drafting on those risks. They are the priority. I leave the poorly drafted severability and the reasonable efforts clauses alone.

How Jerks Jeopardize Negotiations

This contract tip is about how jerks jeopardize negotiations.

Negotiations are a partnership in which each side is working together to find a mutually acceptable deal. Sometimes you do. Sometimes you don't. But being a jerk, getting angry, or grandstanding breaks down the trust and alliance needed to reach agreement.

Some time ago, I was negotiating a difficult deal. Despite starting very far apart, we had reached consensus on everything except a few issues.

The business lead and I had a quick meeting before what was supposed to be our final call. We discussed the risks and decided to concede all remaining points. When we got on the call, the lawyer and business lead for the other side started out the call with a tirade, hurling insults and threats, and angrily demanding that we accept their final edits without change.

My business lead immediately terminated the negotiations and we moved on to engage the next vendor for the needed supply. Why? Because the vendor revealed its true colors. Their behavior didn't reflect our company's values.

They were not people with whom we wanted to do business.

In my experience, you will consistently get better deals if you are considerate and keep an open mind.

Don't be the jerk.

How to Ask for Changes to Your Contract

This contract tip is about negotiating to change an existing contract.

Don't rush into your asks. Take time with your pacing and be thoughtful in your tone.

I was reminded of this approach by how the director of my bookkeeping firm recently asked to increase the fee. He's a negotiating genius.

His first email asked if I would be open to receiving a proposal for an increase. He explained in that email that his firm could afford to provide raises to the staff only if clients agreed to small increases.

Here's why his technique works so well.

He didn't just tell me they were increasing the fee, which would have put me on the defensive. Instead, he first asked if I would be open to a proposal. It gave me time to acclimate to the idea.

He gave me an emotional reason to say yes. He personalized what saying no would mean to Rajeev, the person who takes such good care of me.

He structured it so my first response would be an easy yes. I'd be rude not to receive a proposal. It created a mindset shift that I had agreed, making a yes to the higher price more likely.

He didn't tell me the specific amount in the first ask. He started a dialogue before introducing the exact number.

(And yes, I did approve the increase.)

CHAPTER 14

PRICE AND PAYMENT

Drafting Payment Terms

This contract drafting tip is about payment terms.

Almost all businesses need an invoice to make a vendor payment. The problem is that many contracts don't properly address that requirement.

Typical contracts say: "Buyer will pay Seller X within 30 days of the Effective Date." Or "Buyer will pay Seller X per widget within 30 days of delivery." These contracts later say, "Seller will send Buyer invoices at [email address]."

Notice that the triggering event (here Effective Date or delivery) is a condition for payment, but the invoice submission is not.

Every commercial contract should include two conditions for payment: receipt of Seller's invoice AND the triggering event. So "Buyer will pay Seller the price within 30 days after the later of Buyer's receipt of the invoice or Seller's delivery of the widget." Or "Seller will invoice Buyer no earlier than the delivery of the widget. Buyer will pay the invoice within 30 days."

Make sure the Buyer's obligation to pay does not kick in unless it has an invoice AND the event has occurred.

It is in both parties' best interest to make sure payment terms are clear and reflect actual business practices.

How to Draft the Amount Payable

This contract tip is about how to draft the amount payable provision.

At first blush, it may seem straightforward. "Buyer pays Seller X." What's complicated about that? In practice, there are lots of nuanced edits you can make to improve your client's position.

Here are three common drafting approaches for these provisions:

1. Introductory clause. Sellers may add that payment is consideration for both services and rights granted. This helps if the seller expects payment even if it doesn't perform all the services. Buyers want the fee to only apply to services and make the performance of all services an explicit condition precedent to the buyer's payment.

2. Reimbursement of expenses. Sellers may include a broad reimbursement for any costs and expenses without restriction. Buyers avoid the seller's approach, as it gives the seller the right to add a lot of extras to the fees. Buyers instead add a no reimbursement language and a statement that the fee is the only thing seller can charge.

3. Fee increases. Sellers may include a mechanism to increase the price, especially if the contract term extends out multiple years. Buyers prefer a fixed price for the entire contract term, no matter how long it lasts.

Dealing with Price Change

This contract tip is about dealing with price changes.

While some contracts include fixed prices, others must have a more flexible approach to deal with changing quantities and types of work.

Here are three things that the parties can add to clarify the fluctuating costs:

1. Require preapproval of some expenses or any that cost more than $X. Many contracts with flexible pricing preapprove related costs and expenses up to a certain dollar threshold. But above that, the parties should be a conversation.

2. Include prices for any out-of-scope services. If the contract says that you must use the seller to repair, update, or do anything else for the product, make sure you include the price for those services. Otherwise, the buyer may be stuck paying unreasonable fees.

3. Include pricing adjustments to address future changes. No one has a crystal ball to know what will happen. When you don't know what you may need or when, consider adding a price adjustment mechanism. These can reflect inflation, actual use of the product, or other variables.

Both parties benefit from having contract mechanisms that prevent surprises.

CHAPTER 15

PURCHASE ORDERS

Purchase Orders as Stand-Alone Binding Contracts

This contract tip is about purchase orders as stand-alone binding contracts.

I often hear people say, "We don't have a contract with that vendor. We just use purchase orders." So, there is no confusion, there may be no signature, but they do have a contract. A contract exists when there is an offer, acceptance, and consideration (value exchanged). No signature is required.

Each purchase order is either the offer or the acceptance (unless of course there is a signed master or umbrella agreement that says otherwise). Some purchase orders say that the buyer accepts the offer the vendor made in its quote. Other purchase orders reject the quote and are offers that the vendor can accept or reject.

Whether a purchase order is an offer or acceptance is a very fact-specific question. We look at what the parties said and wrote in conversations, emails, and the purchase order itself. We consider the facts in light of contract law rules around the offer, counteroffer, and rejection. We may even have to look at the mailbox rule ("Please. Not the mailbox rule.").

The conflicting facts and documents sometimes make it hard to figure out the exact terms, but purchase orders are self-contained contracts when they meet the requirements.

How Quotes and Purchase Orders Work

This contract tip clarifies how quotes and purchase orders work in the purchasing process.

The seller issues a quote. It describes the goods or services that the seller proposes to sell to the buyer. Quotes may cover single or multiple items. Some quotes are firm, meaning the seller promises to keep the offer open for a limited time. Some quotes are not firm and just list out options.

The buyer issues a purchase order (PO). In most bigger companies, a system called an enterprise resource planner (ERP) generates the PO.

The ERP system has all the data for all aspects of the company's operations. The person creating the PO enters information about the order in the ERP system. They add documents, identify the price and Incoterms, and related details.

When the PO is complete, the person submits it for approval. Once approved, the PO goes to the seller, either manually by email or automatically by the ERP system. When the seller receives the PO, the seller must accept or reject it.

Of course, there are a million other details that go into this process. But that is why procurement folks get paid the big bucks!

Attachments to Purchase Orders

This contract tip is about adding detailed attachments to purchase orders (POs).

In an ideal world, we would have a signed contract with robust specifications and scopes of work for every purchase. But companies often buy some things just using POs.

Ok, we think, can we at least get detailed specifications and scopes of work in every PO? That's not going to happen either. Most companies don't budget the resources for this approach.

The reality is we must triage and decide which POs get more detailed attachments. The easiest way to decide is by cost. But we usually need to consider more factors.

Here's my approach to that triage:

- Look at the public information for what we are purchasing. Does the vendor describe it in detail in its sales documents or on the website? Is there a publicly available warranty that is good enough?

- Look at the vendor. Is this a vendor we know well? I'm less worried about great vendors who consistently make things right regardless of the contract. I require POs with more details for difficult vendors who nickel and dime us.

- Look at our risk. What happens if this product is terrible? Will people get hurt? Will it interfere with our critical business functions?

Purchase Order Acceptance Provisions

This contract tip is about purchase order acceptance provisions.

Most companies use purchase orders to buy goods and services. When a company plans to make repeated purchases from a seller, that buyer and seller may enter into a master agreement. The master agreement will include a provision that lays out the ongoing ordering process.

There are two primary components to the ordering process provisions:

1. How long does the seller have to accept or reject a purchase order?

2. If the seller does not respond within that period, is the purchase order considered accepted or rejected?

The internal business processes of the buyer and seller usually determine how they approach these issues.

Some buyers rely on enterprise resource planning software to manage purchase orders. These companies may not be set up to manage and track an affirmative acceptance of each purchase, so they rely on "deemed acceptance."

Some sellers lack the structure to reliably reject every purchase order received. They rely on "deemed rejection" language.

Like most things in contracts, we must carefully draft this provision to reflect the business realities of both sellers and buyers.

Signing Quotes and Incorporating in Purchase Orders

This contract tip is about signing quotes and incorporating quotes into purchase orders (POs).

PO forms always provide that the customer's terms control. But the situation gets muddy when you add the vendor's quote to the PO.

Here's how that usually plays out. The customer receives a vendor quote describing the commercial and technical details. The customer's purchasing lead then signs the quote, attaches the quote to the PO, or states in the notes section of the PO that it incorporates the quote.

Seems simple enough. What could go wrong?

A lot.

Because most quotes provide that the vendor's terms govern all sales and the vendor rejects any different terms in the customer's PO. So now you have a PO that in one place says the customer's terms govern and, in another place, says the vendor's terms govern. Yes, we can try to sort it out by diving into the law on offer, counteroffer, rejection, and acceptance.

But what we know for certain is it is now a mess.

The BETTER way for customers to minimize this confusion is to NEVER refer to or incorporate a vendor's quote into a PO. Instead, type or cut and paste just the essential technical and commercial terms from the quote into the notes section of the PO.

CHAPTER 16

RISK

Using Contract Risk Management

Today's contract tip is about using managing risk in our contract drafting and negotiations.

Risk management focuses on identifying, analyzing, and responding to risk. We can use its framework to direct how we manage our contract risks.

My favorite definition of risk is "the effect of uncertainty on our objectives." The elements provide a great process to decide how to mitigate and manage the risks in your deals.

We start by identifying our objectives. We only are at risk of missing the goals that we set. If your goals do not include taking delivery in two weeks, you are not at risk of failing it.

We then identify the uncertainty. What could go wrong? What could happen to interfere with achieving your objectives? Each deal has different danger zones.

Then we evaluate the effect of those uncertainties on our objectives.

This step requires we look at likelihood and impact.

By doing so, we can systematically evaluate how to "right size" our focus and discussion while we negotiate our contracts.

We need to identify and focus mainly on the high impact risks, especially the high likelihood ones. We should worry less about the low impact risks, especially the low likelihood ones.

Risk management provides the path to figure all this out.

Aligning Risk in Your Supply Chain

This contract tip is about the importance of aligning risk allocations between you, your vendors, and your customers.

The bilateral contracts that you are negotiating are only one piece of a very big supply puzzle.

Take the example of a solar module. A material manufacturer sells its goods to a manufacturer of a component piece, which then sells the completed piece to a module manufacturer, which then sells the module to a solar company, which then sells the module to a consumer.

You can recreate this same chain of supply for every good and service out there. At every step, something could go wrong that ends up causing the good or service to fail or, in some cases, injure someone.

As contract lawyers, we focus on the deal in front of us. What is the allocation of risk between these two parties in this deal?

But sometimes we need to step back. How are we managing risk across the entire life cycle of our products or services?

Companies that only focus on risk in their bilateral contracts may find themselves holding more risk than they should when something goes wrong. Step back sometimes and evaluate your risk at a high level. You may see issues that you would not see when you only focus on bilateral contracts.

CHAPTER 17

TERMINATION

Termination for Bankruptcy

This contract tip is about provisions that grant rights to terminate following a bankruptcy filing.

They are not enforceable in the U.S.

"What? Are you kidding?" (No, I am not.)

"But they are in every contract! Why do we include an unenforceable provision?"

I'll get to that, but first, here's a quick background.

The U.S. Bankruptcy Code gives the court handling the bankruptcy case broad authority over the bankrupt entity. That authority supersedes any contract provisions. Section 365(e)(1) provides that only the court can decide which executory contracts (ones not yet performed) are assumed (confirmed), rejected (canceled), or terminated.

So why do we still include these provisions? These are the reasons I've heard:

- Why not? (Not a great reason.)

- The law might change. (A bad reason.)

- It only applies if a party files bankruptcy. These provisions also include other triggers short of bankruptcy.

There are VERY narrow exceptions for personal service, securities, and financial market contracts.

The widely accepted and standard practice is to include them even though they are unenforceable. I do. Just remember that once a party files bankruptcy, you are pretty much stuck.

Terminating Agreements Before Expiration

This contract tip is about terminating agreements before their expiration.

When a client asks me to help with termination, I first figure out what is really going on before I provide any advice.

Here are the five things I ask:

1. "What is the reason you want to terminate?" I always start with why. Knowing the true motivation is critical for structuring my advice. Keep in mind the reason may not be a breach.

2. "What do you want?" I may be able to time or structure things to meet the clients' needs.

3. "What happened?" I find out as much as I can about what led to the situation. I want to know the favorable and not so favorable facts.

4. "What is documented internally about this matter?" Figuring out what documentation exists and what it says helps me evaluate our position in case there is a dispute.

5. "What did you tell the counterparty?" I want to know what the client said orally and in writing to the other side.

After I learn all the above, I analyze the contract and other documents considering those facts. We can't advise on a client's rights and the risks until we know what is going on. And sometimes once we do know, it becomes very clear that the next step is to turn the whole thing over to a litigator.

Termination Dates in Commercial Contracts

This contract tip is about termination dates in commercial contracts.

Most commercial contracts take a simple approach to termination. You breach, we give you 30 days to cure, and the contract automatically terminates at the end of the 30-day period if you didn't cure. This works for some deals, but not for others. If the parties have an intertwined relationship, having a contract suddenly stop can be a disaster for the non-defaulting party.

Consider whether you should include other provisions that make the transition easier. Many contracts include a last buy right to buy up enough supply to get the customer through.

Others have transition services or supply, so the seller must keep delivering for some period after termination. There is another approach that I don't see often in commercial contracts but works really well sometimes.

Give the non-defaulting party the right to select a different termination date within 30 days of the cure period's expiration.

Always think about the end game for your contracts. Make sure to give your client or company time to get their business in order following the contract's end.

Preliminary Steps Before Termination

This contract tip is about four preliminary steps before you terminate a contract.

When a vendor relationship is headed in a bad direction, you should prepare for a successful termination process.

Here are four steps I recommend:

1. Discuss with your team the need to stay in compliance with your contract obligations. Business and technical teams may not realize how important it is that your company doesn't breach the agreement.

2. Make sure you have sent at least one written notice to the counterparty about the factual issues causing the concerns. The first notice should never be the termination notice.

3. Review existing internal documentation about the problem. Figure out what has been communicated to the other side about the problems. Identify any inconsistencies and gaps in that communication. Evaluate whether you should provide more feedback to the vendor before things advance.

4. Develop a transition plan for the vendor. Meet with your team to make sure they are clear on how the transition will work. Coordinate your timing for the termination with whatever vendor will replace them. Figure out if you have rights to wind down in the existing contract before termination.

Chapter 18

TITLE AND RISK OF LOSS

Transfer of Title in Goods

This contract tip is about transferring title in goods.

Many lawyers don't realize it, but U.S. law says that title to goods cannot pass after delivery no matter what the contract says. So much of U.S. contract law gives the parties autonomy to agree to whatever terms they want. But that freedom does not apply to passage of title.

As background, every U.S. state has enacted the same core statute covering the sale of goods called Uniform Commercial Code (UCC). Section 2-401 of the UCC provides that title passes to buyer when seller completes its delivery obligations. The buyer and seller can agree in the contract to pass title earlier than that, but not later.

Before the UCC, the U.S. followed the rule found in most other countries that a seller can retain title after delivery. Sellers around the world rely on this right to repossess goods when the buyer doesn't pay.

The UCC replaced that approach with a new concept - a security interest. If the contract provides for seller to keep title after delivery, the UCC automatically converts the seller's interest in the goods at delivery into a security interest.

Title to Goods Transferring at Delivery

This contract tip is about title to goods rule under Uniform Commercial Code Section 2-401.

If the contract says that a seller retains title after delivery, Section 2-401 of the UCC automatically converts the seller's interest in the goods to a security interest.

Here's how that plays out in the real world.

The seller thought it had title but doesn't. Think how that could affect a company's operations. For example, are the statements to lenders or potential investors about a company's assets inaccurate? It is not a good thing.

The inverse is true for buyers. If it has title but is not reflecting that status in its internal records, then its records are wrong. Also bad.

Another big problem is that sellers are unlikely to take the proper steps to perfect the security interest when they don't realize that is what they have.

Perfection is a process to make the claim stronger compared to others. Perfection requires registering the security interest with the right U.S. state and within the required time. Otherwise, the security interest is unperfected, and the seller's rights will be secondary to those with perfected security interests.

Avoid this mess. Have title pass at delivery.

Three Key Concepts Around Risk of Loss

This contract tip covers three key concepts around risk of loss.

We often address risk of loss and title together but mean different things. Risk of loss is about which party has financial responsibility for any damage or destruction of the goods. Title is about which party legally owns the goods.

Make sure that you address risk of loss only once in a contract. If you have a sentence that says risk of loss passes at a certain moment and then specify the applicable Incoterm, you have risk of loss in there twice.

Incoterms include risk of loss. If you feel compelled to do so or your counterparty insists on including both a sentence and the Incoterm, just be 100% sure that both have risk of loss pass at the same moment.

It is ok to have title and risk of loss pass at different moments. It is not as common but sometimes we structure it that way for a business purpose.

Some consignment contracts will have the seller keep title of the spare parts stored at a buyer's warehouse but say that buyer has risk of loss for those spare parts. If the warehouse burned down, we'd look to buyer's insurance, not seller's, even though seller had title.

CHAPTER 19

TRAINING AND SKILL DEVELOPMENT

Learning How to Draft Contracts

This contract tip is for anyone trying to learn how to draft contracts.

A new lawyer asked me how to learn what contracts should say. He wanted to know how we take a template and make it into something our clients sign.

Here are three steps I recommend to figure it out:

1. Always start with the deal.

Ask questions until you fully understand the details about the services or product and their use, key risks, and so forth. You can't protect the client if you don't understand the transaction. Don't be shy or think you are imposing.

2. Learn about the words we use in contracts.

Become an expert at grammar. Use programs that proofread your work. Use active tense and precise words. Understand the law so your words reflect it. Use plain English where you can but not at the expense of enforceability or legal concepts.

3. Figure out the nuances.

Why this word and not that one? When do we use the Incoterm EXW instead of DDP and why? When do we insist on including a copyright license to create derivative works? Learn to read what differentiates one deal from another and how to expand and contract your client's risk.

What Makes Someone a Great Contract Lawyer

This contract tip is about what makes someone a great contract lawyer.

We do not become great because we follow academic instructions on how to write each contract provision. If that were true, we could be replaced tomorrow with an artificial intelligence contract drafting program.

We do not become great because we memorize the law and know the applicable statutes. If that were true, we would task contract negotiations to law school professors.

Technical drafting skills and knowledge of the law are important. But what really differentiates the great contract lawyers is that they understand the psychology part of it.

They know what their counterparts are thinking, what is important to them, how best to communicate with them, and how to build enough rapport to reach an agreement.

Great contract lawyers know how to apply their knowledge of drafting techniques to make edits that persuade the counterparty.

They know which words to include or omit from a tactical perspective, not just an academic one.

They know how to read the other side to decide when to hold fast and when to concede.

If you want to become a great contract lawyer, don't just focus on the words and the law. You also need to focus on understanding the people involved and their motivations.

Being Careful with Your Legal Advice

This contract tip is about being careful with your legal advice.

Always start with why. Why is this person asking you this question at this moment? Sometimes it is obvious. But whenever it is not, I ask a lot of questions before I give any advice.

Here's an example of why. Many years ago, I was stopped in a hallway by someone from the finance department. I worked often with the team to assess warranty reserves and finance issues. The person said, "What does it mean if an account is listed in the name of a trustee?" I was in a rush, so I gave a sentence or two explaining the basic concept. Then I kept walking.

Two weeks later, I arrived at a meeting with finance leadership. They were planning to restate the financials for the business unit because of my off-hand two sentence answer in the hall that day.

Luckily, they had set up this meeting with me before pulling the trigger. I gave a detailed explanation of the concept in the context of the relevant facts. We all agreed that there was no need to restate the financials.

It was a very powerful lesson for me.

Since then, I don't answer random questions unless I first find out the background on why they are asking lawyers.

Contract Errors = Not Enough Contract Training

I believe many common contract drafting and negotiating errors result from incomplete training.

Contract skills come from understanding the nuances. Which word to use when. What do you revise, leave alone, or delete altogether. You don't learn the answers in law school. You learn over time by working on #contracts and getting feedback on how to draft and negotiate.

In the U.K. and other common law countries, new lawyers receive this feedback during required practical training programs. But not in the U.S. Here, once law school graduates pass the bar exam, they may work as an attorney, even if they have zero practical experience.

Some are lucky enough to receive great training as part of their jobs. But many are not. Their bosses don't have time to train so they teach a few basics and leave the new lawyer to figure it out.

These lawyers end up learning a lot of their contract skills from the other side of deals. "That lawyer made this argument, which sounds good, so I'll argue it that way too."

The problem is that the argument may be incorrect, as that lawyer learned it from another lawyer, who learned it that same way too. The misunderstandings perpetuate.

The answer? We need better contract skills training.

Evaluating the Different Advice Out There About Contracts

This contract tip is about evaluating the different advice out there about contracts.

My advice to you? Be discerning. There is a free market of contract advice, with little regulation or filter.

Anyone can say anything at any time. We come to our ideas about contracts from our different experiences. Some learned from experience drafting and negotiating for companies and clients, some from litigating contract cases, and others from studying contract case law.

Do not accept my or anyone's ideas and advice about how to draft contracts as facts.

They are not.

They are opinions.

Evaluate what is said with some healthy skepticism.

It seems obvious to say, but just because someone says something in a LinkedIn post, webinar, blog, or book does not make it true. Let's say I wrote an article that said no one should ever use the word "the" in a contract. Later I criticize you for using "the." When you challenge my position, I point to that article I wrote to prove I am right. "See! It says so right there!"

The logic makes no sense in that sentence and it should make no sense with any other debate on any subject.

Labeling an opinion as a rule does not mean that it is one.

Decide for yourself what makes sense.

Baby Steps to Learning Contracts

Have you seen the movie What About Bob? If you haven't, you must. It is one of my favorites.

It stars Bill Murray as Bob Wiley, a very confused and needy patient of his therapist Dr. Leo Marvin, who is played by Richard Dreyfuss. In the movie, Dr. Marvin promotes his book Baby Steps.

This technique sets small reasonable goals for yourself to do one at a time.

I realized that Baby Steps is how I learn about contracts. I find some time and pick a contract issue challenging me like warranty remedies or cross border tax issues. I then dive deep. I read every blog and article, watch every video, and explore every book section that I can find on that one narrow issue.

As contract lawyers, we are technicians first. We are and need to stay experts in the practice of writing, revising, and negotiating contracts. That can feel overwhelming when there are thousands of contract topics to learn.

If it feels like too much, just remember Dr. Leo Marvin. "Baby steps."

**By the way, Charles Korsmo, the actor who played Dr. Marvin's son Siggy, got a physics degree from MIT, graduated from Yale Law School, worked at Sullivan & Cromwell, and now teaches at Case Western Reserve School of Law. How cool is that?

CHAPTER 20

WORKING WITH CONTRACTS

Contracts are Business Stories

When I read a contract, I read a story.

The recitals start us off with an introduction to the characters and challenges. "Once upon a time, there was a Seller who had a business making shoelaces and a Buyer who has a business selling shoes that need shoelaces. Buyer and Seller agree to a sale of shoelaces on the terms in this agreement."

Then the contract starts developing the characters and the background. We learn about things the characters need to happen for a happy ending. "Seller shall deliver one box of 1,000 shoelaces to Buyer's warehouse by September 15, 2020 and Buyer will pay $25 for the shoelaces within 30 days after receipt of Seller's invoice."

But then, just when everything seems to be fine, the story becomes dark and talks about what happens when things don't go as planned. "If Seller does not deliver on time or the shoelaces fall apart, Buyer may terminate the contract and sue for all the different types of damages."

Contracts even have their own version of "The End." It is the entire agreement provision explaining that what you just read is the entire story as agreed to by Seller and Buyer.

Next time you read a contract, think about what story it tells.

Managing Your Mindset with a Heavy Workload

This tip is about the constant challenge of far more work than in-house lawyers and professionals can do.

When I was in-house, I'd find myself feeling sad, angry, and frustrated over my inability to tackle all the work on my plate. I'd think "There is no way I can do all this. Don't they know I'm only one person?!" I'd get more upset, which made it even harder to get the work done. Surviving a stressful job depends on your mindset.

I became more Zen about my workload after I reached these two realizations.

First, I accepted that the company's staffing decisions created my workload imbalance. The company could hire others to make my job more manageable, but it didn't. I wasn't at fault. All I could do was my best within the staffing levels created by my company.

Second, I realized what an important resource I was for the company. The company takes care of its other resources - maintenance on equipment, upgrades on software - so why was I thinking I should just work until I break? Seeing it that way helped me feel more comfortable taking time out for myself when I needed it, even when things were crazy. It was important for the company that I did.

These mindset tweaks helped me find a lot more serenity amid the chaos of my in-house life.

Why I Love Contracts

I count myself among all the lawyers and professionals in the world who love contracts.

Here's why.

I love the challenge of drafting and negotiating, with each contract different from the next, even if covering the same subject.

I love helping my clients navigate through the process and decide what to demand and ultimately what to concede.

I love the dynamic of dealing with the counterparty, and including all of their legal, business, and technical leads.

I love learning about the business and technology and how I have to understand it in order to properly draft the documents.

I love the complexity of the law, how many subjects we cover, and how legal issues cross over and affect each other.

I love trying to pick the best words that convey what you want to say and will be acceptable to the other side.

I love the arrangement of the words in a logical and well-organized pattern, with no duplicative concepts, and free of sentences that shouldn't be there.

The Honor and Privilege of Helping Clients

I grew up in a family focused on service to others.

My mom worked as a nurse at nursing homes, usually with the most infirm patients who did not have long for this world. She'd come home heartbroken sometimes when a patient died.

To my teenage self, that looked crazy. Why would she put herself through that pain, I thought. Wouldn't she be happier working with people who would recover?

When I asked her about it, she replied that it was her honor and privilege to care for these patients at a time when they needed help the most. It was hard on her but not nearly as hard as it was for them.

That sentiment stayed with me, but I took a very different path. I was drawn to a career in international business and ended up as a lawyer on cross-border technology deals. For a long time, I believed that a life of service was not for me because I worked in the business world.

But I've come to realize that I had in fact chosen a life of service. It is as a lawyer who serves my clients and my community. And now, with my daily contract tips reaching people around the world, I feel like I'm serving even more.

A life of service doesn't always look the same. Whatever our roles, we serve by helping others in their hours of need. And that is our honor and privilege.

CHAPTER 21

OTHER INSPIRATION

While technically not related to contracts, these tips reflect some of the lessons that I've learned over my lifetime. I've included them for those always looking for more peace, balance, and harmony.

Let Your Greatness Shine

Let your greatness shine. That is the best advice I can give everyone for every situation always. It is also the favor that I ask of you on behalf of me and everyone else.

You have a unique perspective and amazing gifts to offer to your work, your community, your friends, and your family.

You need to be yourself, pursue your mission and dreams, and know that you have support from the people around you to do just that.

If you don't have people in your life now who appreciate your awesomeness, do you need to adjust things, so you are around more people who do?

Maybe you can't make a change today or this month or even this year but consider whether you'll be happier finding circumstances that better align with your values and passions.

Unleash yourself so that you can shine up the world. We need you.

Being Afraid Sucks

Being afraid sucks. I've heard people say that fear is a great motivator to help you reach new heights. They embrace it.

I disagree. With fear propelling you, you may go far but your journey will not be as great. Your fear will sap a lot of the joy and peace along the way. I know.

Fear was a big part of my education and my career. I was afraid of not getting into a top college or law school. That pit in my stomach drove me to study harder. At jobs, I was afraid my bosses would discover my incompetence, or I'd screw up some project.

That feeling fed my anxiety and adrenaline, motivating me to get the job done and do it well. So yes, fear helped me succeed, but at what cost?

I look back and see the fear and how it stifled the incredible joy I should have had from achieving academic and professional success. I finally figured all of this out after surviving a lot of heartache.

I happily reached a place in life where I'm finally not afraid all the time. Or, more accurately, a lot less afraid. I'm still just as driven, but now my primary motivators are my passion and my empathy.

And I'll tell you something. Life without being so worried all the time is a hell of a lot more enjoyable and fulfilling.

Emotional Detachment at Work

Are you the victim at work sometimes? Is your boss, coworker, or customer the villain?

Like a lot of people I think, I sometimes fall into this mindset when things became complicated and emotional at work. I was quick to blame everyone else and felt sorry for myself having to deal with all their crap. I'd get emotional about whatever problems I had and focus on how others were to blame. I'd also get worked up trying to rationalize how the problems weren't my fault, even when no one was saying they were.

I can now see how it was just my coping mechanism. I was struggling with something hard and quickly reached for the "it is them, not me" response to make sense of it.

If you find yourself falling into this trap, stop and think it through. What facts do you have to support that they really are the villains? Or are they good people trying their best to get through a difficult situation just like you?

Now when I catch myself having this response, I try to remove as much emotion from my reaction as I can. I then draw on all my empathy and kindness for the people who are the target of my frustration.

Emotional detachment + honest assessment = peace in your heart And I 🖤 peace far more than being the angry victim.

Don't Believe Conventional Wisdom About Success

If you believe social media and conventional wisdom, I should not be successful.

I don't have a morning routine.

I suck at delegation.

I don't plan my week on Sunday and my day before it starts or at the end.

I procrastinate. A lot.

I spend way too much time surfing the Internet, binge-watching Netflix, and playing mindless apps. (That candy is not going to crush itself!)

Every day, people tell us the rules to follow to be productive and successful. I disagree with them.

You know why? They aren't you. They don't get how you work.

Do you think successful people listen to conventional wisdom? They don't. They experiment. They fail. They experiment some more. They totally screw everything up again and start over. They figure out what works for them and pay no mind to the rest.

Don't let social media suggest that your only path is to do things the way that works for other people.

I believe the only universal rules for success are to out-work everyone else and take giant leaps blindfolded when there is no safety net. Because your success won't flow from following conventional wisdom and your failures won't come because you didn't adopt the time-management idea of the day.

You will succeed because you worked hard and allowed the greatness inside you to shine.

You Never Had Control, You Had Anxiety

"You are afraid of surrender because you don't want to lose control. But you never had control; all you had was anxiety."

I discovered this quote by Elizabeth Gilbert around the same time a Big Law partner told me that he wanted to open his own firm like I had but was too scared to take the leap.

Let me tell you. I was scared to death when I opened my firm last year. I was a single mom and the sole support for me and my four teenage sons. I was leaving a great job with a regular paycheck and a 401k and health insurance to do what? Launch a law firm by myself with no clients and no experience running a firm? Was I crazy? This was not a logical or sane thing to do.

But here is the thing. I realized that I would have a lot of fear even if I stayed. I would have the fear of being laid off, the fear of screwing up, the fear of pissing off someone in charge, and so forth.

The truth I found was that I would be afraid no matter what I did. I would never have control of everything that happens to me and that would always make me scared. Once I found peace with my lack of control, I accepted my fear and found the courage to take the leap anyway.

Think about these questions. What is beyond your fear? Is your fear protecting you or preventing you from achieving your best life?

Stay Tuned

Stay tuned. I love this two-word phrase because of how much wisdom is packed into it. I haven't always, but now I intentionally try to live my professional and personal life this way.

Stay tuned in to your life as it now. Track who and what brings you joy, moves you forward, and drags you down. Take time to reflect. Honestly acknowledge and evaluate your mindset and circumstances.

Stay tuned in to what pulls you. Notice if you feel yourself wanting to do that thing or change your life in that way. Your soul is telling you where to go next. Listen to that inner voice so you keep moving in the right direction.

Stay tuned in to your family, friends, and coworkers. While you are busy working on your challenges, how are the people you love doing? Focus on how you can support and help those closest to you.

Stay tuned in to the world. As much as we're tempted by the idea of ignoring all the conflict and strife, we need to stay present and participate. It is our responsibility as citizens to bring our values to our communities and our countries.

And finally, always stay tuned for what is to come. Today is not the end of your story. It is just part of the journey. Stay mindful that what you are experiencing today is helping you get to where you need to be lawyers.

INDEX

THE END

Made in the USA
Las Vegas, NV
03 August 2021